YORK NOTES

Pygmalion

George Bernard Shaw

Notes by
David Langston & Martin J. Walker

  Longman   York Press

YORK PRESS
322 Old Brompton Road, London SW5 9JH

ADDISON WESLEY LONGMAN LIMITED
Edinburgh Gate, Harlow,
Essex CM20 2JE, United Kingdom
Associated companies, branches and representatives throughout the world

First published 1997

ISBN 0–582–31454–2

Designed by Vicki Pacey, Trojan Horse
Illustrated by Susan Scott
Map by Neil Gower
Phototypeset by Gem Graphics, Trenance, Mawgan Porth, Cornwall
Produced by Longman Asia Limited, Hong Kong

ONTENTS

Preface   4

PART ONE

INTRODUCTION   How to Study a Play   5
                George Bernard Shaw's Background   6
                Context & Setting   9

PART TWO

SUMMARIES   General Summary   13
                Detailed Summaries, Comment,
                Glossaries & Tests   16
                Act I   16
                Act II   21
                Act III   27
                Act IV   33
                Act V   37

PART THREE

COMMENTARY   Themes   44
                Structure   47
                Characters   49
                Language & Style   53

PART FOUR

STUDY SKILLS   How to Use Quotations   55
                Essay Writing   56
                Sample Essay Plan & Questions   59

PART FIVE

CULTURAL CONNECTIONS
                Broader Perspectives   62
Literary Terms   63
Test Answers   64

PREFACE

York Notes are designed to give you a broader perspective on works of literature studied at GCSE and equivalent levels. We have carried out extensive research into the needs of the modern literature student prior to publishing this new edition. Our research showed that no existing series fully met students' requirements. Rather than present a single authoritative approach, we have provided alternative viewpoints, empowering students to reach their own interpretations of the text. York Notes provide a close examination of the work and include biographical and historical background, summaries, glossaries, analyses of characters, themes, structure and language, cultural connections and literary terms.

If you look at the Contents page you will see the structure for the series. However, there's no need to read from the beginning to the end as you would with a novel, play, poem or short story. Use the Notes in the way that suits you. Our aim is to help you with your understanding of the work, not to dictate how you should learn.

York Notes are written by English teachers and examiners, with an expert knowledge of the subject. They show you how to succeed in coursework and examination assignments, guiding you through the text and offering practical advice. Questions and comments will extend, test and reinforce your knowledge. Attractive colour design and illustrations improve clarity and understanding, making these Notes easy to use and handy for quick reference.

York Notes are ideal for:
- Essay writing
- Exam preparation
- Class discussion

The authors of these Notes are: David Langston MA, an English teacher and examiner at GCSE and 'A' level, who has written and contributed to GCSE textbooks; and Martin J. Walker, an English teacher, journalist and NEAB examiner, who has worked on the GCSE examinations in English and English Literature since 1988 and is now a senior examiner.

The text used in these Notes is the Longman Literature edition, edited by Jacqueline Fisher (Longman, 1991).

Health Warning: **This study guide will enhance your understanding, but should not replace the reading of the original text and/or study in class.**

PART ONE

INTRODUCTION

HOW TO STUDY A PLAY

You have bought this book because you wanted to study a play on your own. This may supplement classwork.

- Drama is a special 'kind' of writing (the technical term is 'genre') because it needs a performance in the theatre to arrive at a full interpretation of its meaning. When reading a play you have to imagine how it should be performed; the words alone will not be sufficient. Think of gestures and movements.

- Drama is always about conflict of some sort (it may be below the surface). Identify the conflicts in the play and you will be close to identifying the large ideas or themes which bind all the parts together.

- Make careful notes on themes, characters, plot and any sub-plots of the play.

- Playwrights find non-realistic ways of allowing an audience to see into the minds and motives of their characters. The 'soliloquy', in which a character speaks directly to the audience, is one such device. Does the play you are studying have any such passages?

- Which characters do you like or dislike in the play? Why? Do your sympathies change as you see more of these characters?

- Think of the playwright writing the play. Why were these particular arrangements of events, these particular sets of characters and these particular speeches chosen?

Studying on your own requires self-discipline and a carefully thought-out work plan in order to be effective. Good luck.

Who was this Shaw, G.B.S., George Bernard Shaw (he didn't like the George) who entertained and scandalised Victorian and Edwardian London with his wit, his socialist politics and his love affairs? A vegetarian and teetotaller, he was one of those rare people who have given birth to an adjective – 'Shavian' like 'Machiavellian', 'Napoleonic' and 'Byronic'.

'Shavian' as applied to wit, for example, is associated with a playful, fanciful, though sharply and often cruelly satirical (see Literary Terms) intelligence. Shaw was a man who boldly tackled the hypocrisies and injustices which he saw around him and, like so many gifted Irishmen, he used the English language like a deadly keen rapier to prick the pomposities and prejudices of the self-satisfied British establishment.

Early life

Shaw was born in Dublin in 1856 and died in Hertfordshire in 1950. His father was a civil servant, merchant and secret drinker. His mother was a music teacher and a talented singer. Shaw hated school but had an insatiable appetite for knowledge and could not remember a time when he could not read.

After an unhappy start as a clerk, he moved to London in 1876 determined to become a successful writer. His mother, who was teaching music there, supported him for three years while he tried to achieve success as a novelist.

Politics

In London he became interested in economics and politics after hearing the American Henry George and he involved himself in debating societies, becoming a popular public speaker.

Shaw joined the Fabian Society, a Socialist group which included several prominent intellectuals and he soon became a member of its executive and one of its leading speakers. He campaigned vigorously for its platform of gradual social change through practical and rational methods and education. He supported women's suffrage and anti-colonial movements. *The Intelligent Woman's Guide to Socialism and Capitalism* (1928) is a good introduction to his social and political philosophy.

Playwright

Shaw was always provocative and his plays were often concerned with uncomfortable issues. *Widowers' Houses* dealt with slum landlords and *Mrs Warren's Profession* with prostitution. 'My business …' said Shaw, 'is to chasten morals with ridicule'. He was not apologetic about teaching and preaching and in the Preface to *Pygmalion* he takes pride in being didactic, indeed he claims that great art can never be anything else.

At the beginning of the new century Shaw was the leading figure in the world of drama. He had gained great respect as a critic and he expounded the view that the dramatist should be primarily concerned with social issues and a new and challenging approach to morality.

Pygmalion

Shaw conceived the idea for *Pygmalion* in 1897; by the time it was first performed in London in 1914, he had become a successful critic, political writer and campaigner, showman and dramatist. He believed that there was a creative force within each of us struggling towards improvement and perfection (even in a poor flower girl). His own creative force was still active when he was ninety-four.

As a dramatist Shaw was not content to leave the staging of his plays to others. He took an active, often contentious part in directing. He was also a capable businessman. He suggested that plays should be put on in London for a limited season of six weeks and then tour the provinces before returning to London. He believed that this would extend the life of many plays and increase their profitability.

When *Pygmalion* was first performed in London it was a huge hit. This was especially welcome as Shaw had been going through a dull and unexciting period.

Shaw had very clear ideas about the staging of his plays.

Shaw wanted the renowned Mrs Patrick Campbell to play the leading part. He had seen her play Ophelia in *Hamlet* seventeen years before and had conceived the idea then of her playing a cockney flower girl.

He did not dare offer her the part directly as he knew she would think it beneath her dignity so he invited her to a reading of the play and through a combination of trickery and flattery she was persuaded to take on the part of Eliza.

Shaw, always susceptible to women's charms, was swept off his feet by the great actress and, according to himself, 'was in love for nearly thirty-five hours'. Although he was sharp enough to prevent her taking over the running of the play, he wrote many love letters to his 'glorious white marble lady'.

Shaw had problems with both his leads. Mrs Patrick Campbell and Sir Herbert Beerbohm Tree, the actor-manager who played Higgins, were both very successful but set in their ways and they did not believe Shaw knew much about acting. Tree could only imagine a hero as being something like Romeo and Mrs Patrick Campbell upset Shaw by muttering her lines in rehearsals and moving the furniture around. Shaw eventually had the furniture screwed down.

However, *Pygmalion* was an enormous success wherever it appeared and whoever played in it.

HISTORICAL BACKGROUND

By the end of the nineteenth century the landed gentry and the country agricultural labourer were in serious decline. Cheap imported food had reduced the importance of British agriculture. By 1911 the population of the United Kingdom had increased by 25 per cent in forty years and over 75 per cent of that population were living in or near towns.

The first working-class MPs

After 1870 basic education was available to all and by the early twentieth century employers were faced with a literate and increasingly organised workforce. The lower classes could no longer be counted on to 'know their place'. Another sign of the decline of the landed gentry was the reduction of the powers of the House of Lords in 1911. On the other hand, members of Parliament in the elected House of Commons were given salaries for the first time. Working-class representatives could now afford to be MPs. Before this politics had generally been a rich man's preserve, often treated as a hobby rather than as a public service.

Strikes

The years 1911 and 1912 saw serious and violent industrial conflict. Soldiers were sent to deal with striking miners and railwaymen and several people were killed.

The Suffragette movement

The Suffragette movement was carrying out a vigorous and often violent campaign for votes for women. There were mass arrests after clashes with police. In June 1913 Emily Davison, a suffragette, was killed when she tried to stop the king's horse in the Epsom Derby.

However, there was some movement in attitudes towards women, who had few rights in law and who were often treated as property, especially in marriage. In November 1912 a Royal Commission on Divorce recommended that men and women should be treated equally by the divorce laws and it called for the grounds for divorce to include habitual drunkenness, cruelty and desertion.

Poor medical care There was still real deprivation and hardship in the country and in 1913 Sir George Newman, the chief medical officer for schools, reported that more than half of the 6 million schoolchildren needed dental treatment, a third were unhygienically dirty and significant numbers suffered from tuberculosis, heart disease and skin complaints. Large families were common and many women died in childbirth.

The origins of the Labour party The Fabian Society was an organisation which encouraged the development and exchange of ideas about social reform and industrial production. It aimed to bring better education, health care and increased prosperity to the majority and to break down class barriers, eventually creating a world community with justice and plenty for all. It was one of the groups which founded the Labour party. Shaw was a leading member and one of their most popular speakers.

THEATRE In the late nineteenth and early twentieth century many people involved in the theatre believed that drama should somehow reveal the truth about life, and show reality. Shaw felt that scientific study of humanity and society, the way people live and relate to each other, should be at the heart of theatrical drama. Like Strindberg (Swedish dramatist 1849–1912) and Ibsen (Norwegian dramatist 1828–1906), Shaw stressed the importance of thought and scientific method. Intelligence was more important than imagination. Reason should come before fancy. Tanner, a character in Shaw's play *Man and Superman*, says, 'the artist's work is to show us ourselves as we really are'. For artist we can read writer or dramatist.

In England, some contemporaries of Shaw, like J.M. Barrie of *Peter Pan* fame, John Galsworthy, W. Somerset Maugham and James Bridie, wrote well-intentioned but dull dramas of ideas. Theatre audiences in London were generally upper middle class and women were in the majority.

In Ireland, the poet W.B. Yeats had helped found the Irish National Theatre Society in 1901 and together with the Abbey Theatre Company it produced an upsurge of realistic and romantic national drama, often very controversial and even provoking violent protest. Yeats wrote for the company and it also produced two dramatists whose work has survived the test of time: Sean O'Casey and J.M. Synge.

Popular entertainment

The popular taste in entertainment was for music hall variety shows with comic turns, acrobats and sentimental ballads. The first Royal Command Performance was held in December 1912 at the Palace Theatre before King George V and Queen Mary. On the bill were popular acts like Little Titch, Vesta Tilley and the Scottish comedian Harry Lauder who was a special favourite with the king. There was also a novelty Ragtime Band from America.

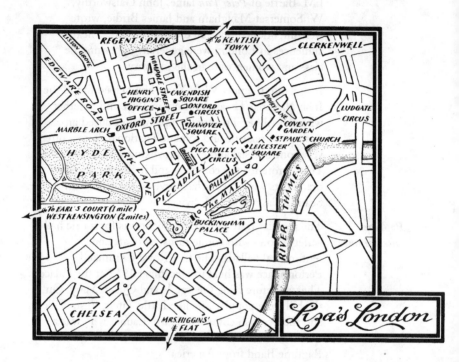

PART TWO

SUMMARIES

GENERAL SUMMARY

Act I   On a summer evening, several people are sheltering from a heavy rainstorm under the front of a church in Covent Garden market. Freddy, an upper-middle-class young man, has been sent to find a cab to take his mother and sister home after a visit to a theatre. When he returns without one he is sent off again and bumps into a poor flower girl who calls him 'Freddy'. Freddy's mother wants to know how this common girl knows her son's name. She discovers that the girl calls all strange men 'Freddy' or 'Charlie'.

Eliza, the flower girl, tries to sell some flowers to an elderly military gentleman and one of the other people sheltering warns her to look out as someone is taking notes. This causes quite a fuss as Eliza is worried about being mistaken for a prostitute and protests loudly that she is a 'good girl'.

The note taker is Professor Higgins, a phonetician, an expert in the study of the sounds people produce when they speak. He is taking notes as he has a great interest in dialects and accents. Higgins boasts that he could train Eliza to speak like a duchess in three months. The military gentleman, Colonel Pickering, is delighted to discover the man's identity as he has come to England to meet Professor Higgins. He too is an expert in dialects and specialises in Indian languages. Likewise, Higgins has been hoping to meet Pickering. They go off to have supper and discuss phonetics.

Act II   Next morning, Eliza arrives at Higgins's house. She wants him to teach her to speak like a duchess so that she can get a job in a shop. Pickering is there and he bets that Higgins can't do it. Higgins accepts the challenge and orders his housekeeper to scrub Eliza and to get her some new clothes.

Eliza's father, Alfred Doolittle, a dustman, arrives hoping to get money from Higgins in exchange for his daughter. He eventually settles for five pounds. Soon Higgins starts to teach Eliza.

Act III   After some time Higgins takes Eliza to his mother's house to see if she will pass for a lady among his mother's guests. The guests are the Eynsford Hills, the family who were waiting for a cab in the rain at the beginning of the play but they do not recognise Eliza as the poor flower girl. Freddy, the son, is fascinated by her. Eliza speaks with a very correct accent but she surprises the guests by her lurid description of her aunt's death. Afterwards, Mrs Higgins points out that Eliza is not yet ready for high society and that Henry may have created a problem. What about Eliza's future?

Act IV   Before the period of the bet (now extended to six months) is over, Eliza has been a great success at an embassy ball. Back at Higgins's house, the two men are celebrating 'their' success, forgetting Eliza's part altogether and they are shocked and bewildered when she is angry with them. She is worried about her future and feels she has served her purpose and will be cast off.

Eliza leaves the house and meets Freddy Eynsford Hill who is in love with her and has been hanging around outside. They kiss and then wander the streets before getting a taxi to Wimbledon Common.

Act V   Next morning, when Higgins discovers that Eliza is missing, he phones the police and goes to his mother's house. He is amazed when she tells him that Eliza is upstairs. Eliza's father arrives to invite Higgins to his wedding. He blames Higgins for making him respectable. Higgins had told a wealthy friend about

Doolittle's interesting ideas about morality and the wealthy friend had left Doolittle a large sum of money.

When Eliza enters, Higgins tries to persuade her to return to his house, assuring her that he treats everyone the same. He says he misses her and suggests that he, Eliza and Pickering could live as equals. Eliza does not agree. She tells him that she is going to marry Freddy as soon as she can support him and goes to her father's wedding with Mrs Higgins.

Afterword   To emphasise there was to be no romantic connection with Higgins, Shaw wrote an afterword which described Eliza's later life, married to Freddy.

Detailed summaries

Act i

[Sheltering from the rain]

A group of people of various sorts are sheltering from a heavy summer rainstorm under the portico of St Paul's church in Covent Garden. It is late evening and the theatres have just emptied.

Two ladies, Mrs Eynsford Hill and her daughter Clara are among the group. They are dressed in formal evening gowns as they have just come from the theatre and they are complaining about the length of time they have been waiting while Clara's brother, Freddy, has been searching for a cab to take them home.

Mrs Eynsford Hill is shocked when the flower girl calls her son Freddy.

When Freddy returns empty-handed they send him off to look again. As he rushes out he bumps into a poor flower girl who is coming in for shelter and damages some of her flowers. As she complains she calls him 'Freddy', which surprises Mrs Eynsford Hill.

Eliza, the flower girl speaks in a very strong cockney dialect when she asks Freddy's mother to pay for the damaged flowers. Shaw says that he will not try to represent the cockney dialect after this speech as it will be too difficult for most readers. He has left us with this example to demonstrate Eliza's dialect and to show what a difficult task Higgins sets himself.

Mrs Eynsford Hill pays for the flowers and asks Eliza how she knew her son's name. Eliza replies that she calls every strange man she meets either 'Freddy' or 'Charlie'.

The Note Taker

Eliza strongly defends her good character.

It is raining harder than ever and an elderly gentleman who seems like a retired army officer takes shelter. Eliza asks him to buy some flowers and a man standing nearby warns her that someone is taking notes. Eliza

Y

The Act introduces us to the nature of Shaw's humour. Higgins addresses the sheltering people in a patronising and hectoring way. As Higgins shows off his brilliance we see Shaw's skill in exposing Higgins's insensitivity. The other characters in this scene are largely caricatures: the ineffectual Freddy, the whining Clara and the loud and raucous cockney flower girl. This is typical of Shaw's witty social commentary and he became well known for his humorous comments on manners.

GLOSSARY   **portico** the front of a building supported by columns
                gumption common sense
                sovereign a pound coin
                half a crown a coin equivalent to twelve and a half new pence
                phonetics the study of speech sounds
                Sanscrit Sanskrit, the ancient literary language of India

TEST YOURSELF (Act I)

 Identify the speaker.

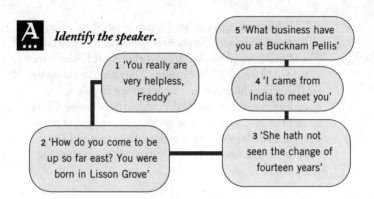

1 'You really are very helpless, Freddy'

2 'How do you come to be up so far east? You were born in Lisson Grove'

5 'What business have you at Bucknam Pellis'

4 'I came from India to meet you'

3 'She hath not seen the change of fourteen years'

Identify the person 'to whom' this comment refers.

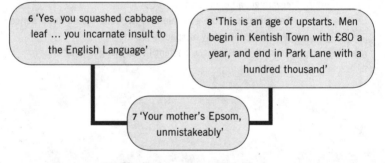

6 'Yes, you squashed cabbage leaf ... you incarnate insult to the English Language'

8 'This is an age of upstarts. Men begin in Kentish Town with £80 a year, and end in Park Lane with a hundred thousand'

7 'Your mother's Epsom, unmistakeably'

Check your answers on page 64.

B **Consider these issues.**

a How Shaw establishes the character of Freddy.

b How Higgins's confidence and rudeness are revealed through his behaviour to the strangers.

c The way in which Shaw brings out Eliza's sense of right and wrong.

d What Higgins's attitude is to those who have made something of themselves but were not born into the middle classes.

e How Clara is revealed as someone brought up to have manners.

ACT II

[HIGGINS'S LABORATORY]

(pp. 20–32) Next morning, Higgins is showing Colonel Pickering round his speech laboratory. The colonel is very impressed.

Mrs Pearce, Higgins's housekeeper, enters and says there is a young woman asking to see him, a very common girl with a dreadful accent. Higgins sees this as an opportunity to demonstrate his recording machine and his phonetic writing systems to Pickering and he tells Mrs Pearce to bring the girl in. The young woman is Eliza. She has made some pathetic attempts to tidy herself and she has come in a taxi. When Higgins recognises her he is no longer interested. He has enough recordings of her particular accent and he tells her to be off.

Higgins is not interested in people unless they are useful to his work.

Eliza protests at this treatment and announces that she has come to have speech lessons because she wants to get a job in a flower shop and she is ready to pay. She expects to be treated more politely when she says this, but Higgins continues in his usual bullying manner. In contrast, Colonel Pickering is very polite to her. When Eliza offers to pay a shilling an hour, Higgins realises that this is quite a large part of her income and he is impressed. He warns her that he would be a strict teacher. When Pickering challenges him to a bet Higgins accepts and claims he will be able to pass Eliza off as a duchess at the ambassador's garden party in six months' time – or even three.

Colonel Pickering is an old-fashioned gentleman who treats Eliza with politeness and kindness.

Higgins tells Mrs Pearce to take Eliza away and clean her and burn her clothes. Eliza does not understand his manner or his humour. He tells Mrs Pearce to keep her in the dustbin at one point. Eventually Pickering asks him to consider Eliza's feelings but Higgins takes no notice. He is only interested in the technical problems he has to deal with if he is to win his bet.

y

Mrs Pearce foresees problems.

Mrs Pearce's instincts tell her that no good will come of Higgins interfering in Eliza's life in this way. She is the only one to ask what will happen to Eliza when the experiment is over. Higgins just makes a joke of it. Mrs Pearce reluctantly takes charge of Eliza and leads her out to be bathed.

COMMENT

Higgins is obsessed with his work and has no time to be polite or considerate of people's feelings.

Eliza shows that she has real ambition to better herself. Her efforts to improve her appearance and her offer of a shilling an hour for lessons are quite touching.

Mrs Pearce has serious doubts about the plan to teach Eliza to speak like a duchess. She thinks Higgins is careless where people are concerned and has not considered the girl's future.

[ELIZA'S BATH, AND ALFRED DOOLITTLE]

(pp. 32–49)
Whilst amused by this we are reminded of Eliza's poverty and ignorance – she thinks bathing is harmful.

Mrs Pearce takes Eliza upstairs to bathe her. Eliza is very reluctant to have a bath and it is obvious that she has never had one before. She has been in the habit of sleeping in her underclothes. However Mrs Pearce is very firm. She gets Eliza into the bath and scrubs her.

Meanwhile Colonel Pickering is questioning Higgins about his morals. He is concerned that Eliza should come to no harm while she is living in Higgins's house. Higgins reassures him that he is as unfeeling as a block of wood where female pupils are concerned. This is ironic (see Literary Terms) as it is true but not in the sense that Higgins intends.

Higgins has little understanding of the impression he makes on other people.

Mrs Pearce returns and asks if she may speak to Higgins. While expressing concern about Eliza's language and dress she gently asks Higgins not to swear in the girl's presence and to mend his table manners. Colonel Pickering is amused. After Mrs Pearce leaves,

Higgins protests that he is much misunderstood. He is convinced that he is a shy, mild sort of person, but we, the onlookers, know otherwise.

Alfred Doolittle (pp. 38–48)
Admire the way Higgins calls Doolittle's bluff.

Mrs Pearce returns to announce that there is a dustman at the door who has come about his daughter. Pickering is concerned but Higgins is confident he can deal with the man even though he expects him to be a 'blackguard'. Higgins is mainly interested in what sort of accent the dustman may have. Alfred Doolittle, Eliza's father enters. He is a bold man with an expressive voice. He obviously hopes to profit from the situation and he demands his daughter, expecting to be bought off. Higgins calls his bluff by telling him to take her. He then accuses Doolittle of plotting blackmail and extortion and threatens to call the police. Doolittle backs down and tries to explain his way out of this but Higgins is adamant and tells Mrs Pearce to fetch Eliza.

Doolittle explains his philosophy. One of the 'undeserving poor'.

Eventually Doolittle says he will settle for £5. He entertains Higgins and Pickering with his speech about being one of the 'undeserving poor' who needs money just as much as the 'deserving poor'. He makes no pretence that he will do anything but spend it on pleasure and amusement. Higgins thinks he could make a good politician or minister of religion out of him if he gave him speech lessons but Doolittle will not hear of it.

He accepts £5 from Higgins and is on his way out when he meets Eliza who is dressed in a Japanese kimono. He does not recognise her and is amazed when she makes herself known to him. Higgins and Pickering are also amazed by the change in Eliza's appearance. Eliza has come to appreciate the washing facilities but was embarrassed by the presence of a mirror in the bathroom. She guesses the purpose of her father's visit and knows how he will use the money.

Doolittle leaves after advising Higgins to use the strap on Eliza if he wants to improve her mind.

Eliza's | Eliza is pleased with the change so far and would like
excitement | to show off to the other flower girls on Tottenham
(p.48–9) | Court Road. She rushes off excitedly when Mrs Pearce says that her new clothes have arrived.

COMMENT | Higgins and Pickering find Doolittle's frankness very entertaining. He has some unusual ideas which interest and amuse the gentlemen. He says the poor cannot afford morals.

The change in Eliza's appearance makes a great impression on the men but her speech is still that of a poor flower girl.

[ELIZA'S FIRST LESSON]

Eliza is quick | Later we are shown Eliza's first speech lesson. She is
to learn | nervous and Higgins makes her more uncomfortable by
(pp.49–50) | striding around the room. Colonel Pickering is gentle with her and gives her encouragement but Higgins is

Eliza is quick to | rude and impatient. However he is pleased by her quick
learn. | response to his instruction. He tells her to go and

practise and Eliza leaves the room in tears. We are told that this is a sample of what Eliza is to suffer for months.

COMMENT We are shown the tension between Eliza's wish to learn and Higgins's insensitivity and impatience tempered by Pickering's calming influence.

By the end of this Act, Eliza's appearance has been transformed and she has made the first steps in changing her speech.

Shaw draws humour from the observation of manners. The concept of a bathroom is totally alien to Eliza; a middle-class audience would have found this amusing. Similarly, when she comes down to meet her father dressed in a silk kimono but does not feel dressed without her hat on, it is comic. The speech lessons bring humour to the play because
- Higgins is interested only in the task in hand and in showing off his skill
- Mrs Pearce is concerned for Eliza and there is humour in the diplomatic way in which she tries to suggest that Higgins's slovenly manners are not a good example
- Pickering is concerned about Eliza's moral welfare
- Higgins says that he is unfeeling where female pupils are concerned, which is true, but not in the way he suggests. He is in fact extremely insensitive

GLOSSARY **laryngoscope** a mirror for internal examination of the throat
Piranesis pictures by Piranesi (1720–78) usually of Roman ruins
mezzotint a type of picture made from an engraving
Monkey Brand a brand of soap
balmies barmies, insane people
copper a boiler for clothes
benzine a solvent

EST YOURSELF (Act II)

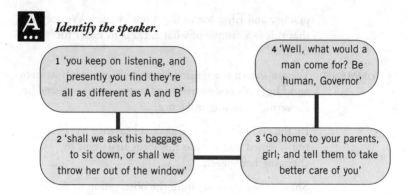

A *Identify the speaker.*

1 'you keep on listening, and presently you find they're all as different as A and B'

4 'Well, what would a man come for? Be human, Governor'

2 'shall we ask this baggage to sit down, or shall we throw her out of the window'

3 'Go home to your parents, girl; and tell them to take better care of you'

Identify the person 'to whom' this comment refers.

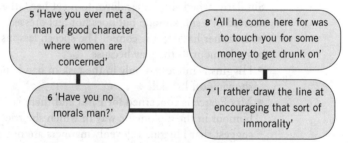

5 'Have you ever met a man of good character where women are concerned'

8 'All he come here for was to touch you for some money to get drunk on'

6 'Have you no morals man?'

7 'I rather draw the line at encouraging that sort of immorality'

Check your answers on page 64.

B *Consider these issues.*

a How genuinely proud Higgins is of his achievements.

b The way in which Pickering treats Eliza when she first appears at Wimpole Street.

c The role of Mrs Pearce in the household.

d The strange morality of Alfred Doolittle and the way in which it appeals to Higgins.

e How Pickering acts as a restraining influence upon Higgins and Doolittle.

f How Eliza's ability to learn quickly points to her future.

ACT III

[E LIZA'S FIRST OUTING]

(pp. 51–66)   Mrs Higgins, Henry's mother, is in her flat on the Chelsea Embankment. She is expecting visitors and is not pleased when Henry bursts in. She knows he always upsets her visitors with his odd manners and tactless remarks. She is rather surprised when he tells her he has invited a common flower girl to her tea party. She is not altogether reassured when Henry tells her he has taught the girl to pronounce words properly but she must try to keep to two topics, health and the weather. He tells his mother about the bet with Pickering.

Note how Higgins is uncomfortable in polite society.   Mrs Higgins's guests are shown in. They are Mrs Eynsford Hill and her daughter Clara, the ladies who were sheltering at Covent Garden at the beginning of the play. Higgins tries to leave but is too late and he is introduced to them. He is barely civil to the ladies and does not hide his impatience.

Colonel Pickering arrives and then Freddy Eynsford Hill. Higgins recognises the Eynsford Hills' voices but cannot remember where he has met them.

Eliza is shown in and is introduced to the company. She is beautifully dressed and pronounces her words carefully and correctly. She makes a strong impression on the company. Mrs Eynsford Hill and her son suggest they have met Eliza somewhere before but it is obvious that they do not recognise her as the poor flower girl. Freddy is fascinated by her.

Note the comic effect Shaw draws from Eliza's account.   Eliza impresses the party by talking very precisely and knowledgeably about the weather, one of her prepared subjects. However she causes some surprise when she speaks about the strange circumstances of her aunt's death. Here she lapses into some cockney slang but Higgins covers up for her by telling the company it is the new fashionable way of speaking. He signals to Eliza that it is time she left and when she has gone he

mischievously encourages Clara Eynsford Hill to
use the new way of speaking when she visits other
houses. Her mother is unsure about this and does
not feel she can ever bring herself to use such
language.

Mrs Higgins
foresees problems.

After the Eynsford Hills leave Higgins asks his mother
what she thinks about Eliza. Mrs Higgins says that
Eliza looks fine but her conversation is not acceptable
and is unlikely to improve in Henry's company. Mrs
Higgins questions Henry and Pickering about Eliza's
position in the house at Wimpole Street. They both
chatter about how useful she is and what a brilliant
student she has been. Mrs Higgins tries to point out
that they have not thought about the problem of Eliza's
future but they brush this aside and go off in good
spirits. Mrs Higgins is exasperated.

COMMENT

Higgins is bored by the company. We see that he is not
a sociable person by his impatient behaviour and his
poor manners.

We have examples from Higgins of the sort of language
that Mrs Pearce complained of. He uses expressions
which are not considered suitable in polite society, e.g.
'damn it', 'what the devil'.

Mrs Higgins tries to keep her son under control by
reminding him of his manners.

The Eynsford Hills are poor upper-middle-class
people desperately trying to keep a foothold in 'good'
society.

Humorous elements in this section include:
- the Eynsford Hills' failure to recognise Eliza as the
  flower girl
- Eliza's carefully pronounced but very technical
  comments on the weather

- Eliza's lurid description of her aunt's death spoken in carefully pronounced upper-class tones but full of lower-class cockney expressions
- Clara, so anxious to be in fashion, that she falls for Higgins's trick
- Mrs Higgins treating her son like a naughty boy

We are again warned that Higgins's experiment may bring problems.

GLOSSARY

Chelsea Embankment a pleasant, fashionable area of London overlooking the River Thames

Morris William Morris (1834–96) English designer, craftsman and poet

Burne Jones (1833–98) painter, friend of Morris and Rossetti

Whistler James Whistler (1834–1903) American artist

Cecil Lawson (1849–82) landscape painter

Inigo Jones (1573–1652) architect and furniture designer

Rossettian in the style of Dante Gabriel Rossetti (1828–82) English painter

estheticism aestheticism, an extreme love of art

ottoman a low upholstered seat without a back

Chippendale an eighteenth-century furniture-maker

at-home day a day set aside for receiving visitors

something chronic (cockney slang) excess

Ripping upper-class slang, expression of approval

[THE EMBASSY]

(pp. 66–71)

Eliza is a sensation at the embassy.

Higgins and Pickering arrive at the embassy party with Eliza. Eliza goes to the cloakroom and Higgins is accosted by an ex-pupil who claims to be an expert in European languages and who is attending the party as an interpreter. This adds another element of excitement to the experiment.

Eliza says she is not nervous as she has dreamed of this

moment many times. She is presented to the
ambassador and his wife as Pickering's adopted
daughter. The ambassador is impressed and tells the
interpreter to find out what he can about Eliza.
The ambassador's wife questions Higgins about her but
he pretends he does not know whom she is talking
about. The interpreter returns and says that Eliza is a
fraud but goes on to say that he believes Eliza to be a
Hungarian princess. Higgins says that she is an
ordinary London girl who has been taught to speak
by an expert but no one will accept this. They prefer
to believe she is a princess and Higgins is left on his
own.

*Shaw is poking
fun at upper-class
gullibility.*

Pickering and Eliza join Higgins and Eliza says she has
had enough of being stared at. She thinks she has been
unsuccessful but Pickering tells her that she has clearly
won the bet for them. Higgins agrees that they should
leave.

COMMENT   After Higgins has succeeded in his experiment and
has won the bet, we are left wondering what happens
next.

It is ironic (see Literary Terms) that the people at the
embassy prefer to believe the ridiculous theory of
Nepommuck, the interpreter, than the truth about
Eliza.

Shaw prepares us for Eliza's reaction in the conversation between Pickering and Higgins. Higgins says 'Let's get out of this. I have had enough of chattering to these fools'. Higgins's reference to Eliza as 'an ordinary London girl out of the gutter' reinforces our view of his insensitivity. This is bound to bring a reaction from Eliza eventually.

The whole embassy scene is full of pompous behaviour and wilful ignorance. Shaw's humour once again is aimed at the pretension of the middle and upper classes.

Eliza is exhausted by her success. Everything seems like an anti-climax (see Literary Terms) now. As in the story of 'The Emperor's New Clothes', the people would prefer to believe the most fantastic version of events rather than believe that they have been fooled.

GLOSSARY   **Pandour** Croatian subject of the Austro-Hungarian Empire
swells (slang) important people
Mrs Langtry Lillie Langtry (1853–1929) actress and famous beauty of her time, one time mistress of the Prince of Wales
Morganatic a marriage between partners who are of unequal rank, the partner of lower rank having no rights of inheritance

A **Identify the speaker.**

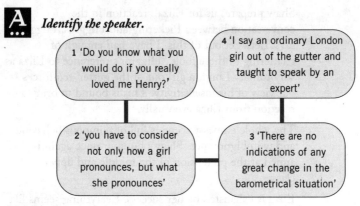

1 'Do you know what you would do if you really loved me Henry?'

4 'I say an ordinary London girl out of the gutter and taught to speak by an expert'

2 'you have to consider not only how a girl pronounces, but what she pronounces'

3 'There are no indications of any great change in the barometrical situation'

Identify the person 'to whom' this comment refers.

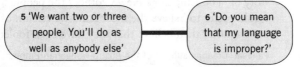

5 'We want two or three people. You'll do as well as anybody else'

6 'Do you mean that my language is improper?'

Check your answers on page 64.

B **Consider these issues.**

a Mrs Higgins is infuriated by her son's behaviour, yet she usually ends up going along with him.

b Eliza seemed much more interesting when she spoke like a flower girl than she does when making small talk about the weather.

c Higgins and Pickering talk about Eliza in her presence, yet behave as though she is simply not there.

d Higgins is far more interested in winning his bet than he seems to be in Eliza's feelings.

e The people at the embassy are very gullible. They are quite ready to accept Nepommuck's silly explanations.

ACT IV

(pp. 72–80)

[ELIZA'S ANGER]

Higgins, Pickering and Eliza arrive back at the Wimpole Street laboratory at midnight. The two men make themselves comfortable and discuss the embassy party. Eliza seems very tired. She is very quiet and obviously has something on her mind. When Higgins thanks God it is all over she flinches. Pickering has enjoyed the experience but Higgins says he has been bored by the experiment for some time. Eliza is visibly annoyed. Pickering goes off to bed after congratulating Higgins on his success. Higgins prepares to follow and gives some domestic instructions to Eliza.

Higgins is unaware of Eliza's growing anger.

When he has left, Eliza throws herself on the floor in a fit of rage and Higgins is shocked when he returns to look for his slippers and has them thrown at him.

She says that now that she has won the bet for him Higgins has no more use for her. Higgins does not know how to deal with this situation and he tries to justify himself by demanding to know if she has been ill-treated by him or anyone else in the house. He suggests that she is suffering from nerves and exhaustion and he does not take her seriously when she says she is worried about what will become of her now.

Eliza has a keen sense of morality.

Higgins has not given this much thought. He patronises her and says that as she is not bad looking she might find a husband to keep her. His mother may help her in this. Eliza rejects the prospect as little better than prostitution. Higgins then says that Colonel Pickering may set her up in a flower shop as he has plenty of money. He will have to pay for her clothes anyway as he has lost the bet. Eliza wants to know if her clothes belong to her or Colonel Pickering as she does not want to accused of stealing when she leaves. Higgins is hurt by this and is angered when Eliza insists that he take charge of her hired jewellery. She returns a ring he had given her and, in a temper, he throws it into the fireplace. Eliza feels some satisfaction when he tells her she has wounded him to the heart. He tries to leave the room with dignity but his temper gets the better of him and he slams the door. Eliza finds the ring but throws it back in the fireplace and goes upstairs in a rage.

COMMENT

Higgins begins to suffer the consequences of his lack of forethought and his insensitivity to Eliza's worries.

Eliza has pride and a strong sense of right and wrong. She shows contempt for middle-class morality when she rejects the idea of finding a husband to keep her.

Higgins shows real emotion for the first time. He has always felt he was in control but his experiment has brought him unexpected complications.

GLOSSARY

La Fanciulla del Golden West an opera by Puccini (1858–1924)

[ELIZA AND FREDDY]

(pp. 80–2)
Eliza takes charge.

Eliza changes into outdoor clothes and leaves the house. She meets Freddy Eynsford Hill in the street. He tells her he has been spending his nights there as it is the only place where he can feel happy. Eliza is touched by his affection and she responds to his kisses. They are moved on by a policeman. She tells him she was on her way to throw herself in the river. They embrace again and are moved on by another policeman. Eventually they come across a taxi and Eliza suggests they drive around until morning. Freddy has no money but Eliza says she will pay. She intends to call on Mrs Higgins in the morning to ask her advice.

COMMENT

Eliza is happy to find affection but she also shows independence and initiative. Freddy is likeable but helpless.

There is humour in the fact that Higgins and Pickering are unaware of Eliza's growing anger as Higgins dismisses her triumph as 'tomfoolery' and can only complain of how hard it has been for him. There is then comic stage business as Eliza throws her slippers at him. This is tinged with pathos (see Literary Terms) as Eliza feels she has been cast aside now that she has served her purpose.

Identify the speaker.

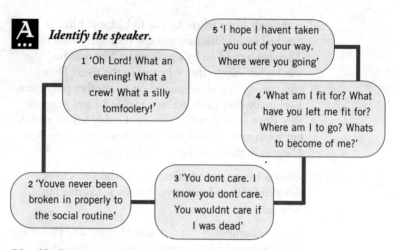

5 'I hope I havent taken you out of your way. Where were you going'

1 'Oh Lord! What an evening! What a crew! What a silly tomfoolery!'

4 'What am I fit for? What have you left me fit for? Where am I to go? Whats to become of me?'

2 'Youve never been broken in properly to the social routine'

3 'You dont care. I know you dont care. You wouldnt care if I was dead'

Identify the person 'to whom' this comment refers.

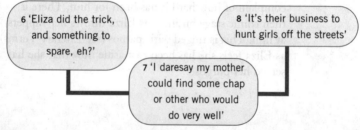

6 'Eliza did the trick, and something to spare, eh?'

8 'It's their business to hunt girls off the streets'

7 'I daresay my mother could find some chap or other who would do very well'

Check your answers on page 64.

B *Consider these issues.*

a How Pickering and Higgins talk about Eliza at the start of Act IV.

b Eliza has been misjudged by the two gentlemen. She would rather be treated decently by them than merely given fine things to wear.

c The way in which Shaw makes the audience side with Eliza.

d Why Eliza is prepared to take up with Freddy, even though he is a fool.

y

ACT V

[LOOKING FOR ELIZA]

(pp. 88–97)   Mrs Higgins is in her drawing room when her maid announces that Henry and Pickering have arrived and are phoning the police. She sends the maid upstairs to warn Eliza of their arrival and to ask her not to come down until sent for.

Higgins bursts in and tells his mother that Eliza has gone. He is very disturbed. One of his complaints is that he relied on her for organising his appointments. Mrs Higgins tells him that Eliza has every right to leave if she pleases. She is annoyed when she finds that Colonel Pickering has phoned the police and reported Eliza as missing.

The maid announces the arrival of a Mr Doolittle, a gentleman. The two men cannot believe it is Eliza's father, the dustman, and guess that it is some respectable relative. However, it is Eliza's father but greatly changed. He is dressed in fine clothes as though on his way to a fashionable wedding. Doolittle complains bitterly to Higgins about this change and blames him as the cause of it. Higgins had jokingly recommended Doolittle as a moral philosopher to a wealthy American. The American had since died and

Doolittle complains of his good fortune.

It is ironic that Doolittle should complain about having been made wealthy.

left Doolittle £3,000 a year provided he gives lectures on Moral Reform.

This good fortune has complicated Doolittle's life. He is now expected to support his unemployed relatives and he will have to learn to speak middle-class English. Mrs Higgins suggests he could turn down the money but Doolittle confesses he does not have the courage to do this. He sees no future for himself as a poor man other than the workhouse and a pauper's grave.

Mrs Higgins suggests that he will now be able to support Eliza but Henry objects, saying that he has paid Doolittle £5 for her. His mother tells him not to be absurd. She reveals that Eliza is upstairs but she makes Henry listen to her while she tries to explain why Eliza was so angry and upset. She says that she herself would have thrown more than slippers at him. Colonel Pickering realises that they have been thoughtless in disregarding Eliza's part in the experiment, but Henry is not impressed and he sulks when his mother makes him promise to behave himself if she sends for Eliza. She asks Doolittle to go out on to the balcony until Eliza has made peace with Henry and Pickering and reminds Henry to behave himself.

Note how cool and dignified Eliza is.

When Eliza enters she behaves in a very calm and dignified way, addressing the two men formally and making polite conversation about the weather. Higgins is annoyed and reminds her that he has taught all these tricks and has created her out of rubbish. He demands that she return home with him.

Eliza makes Higgins squirm by praising Colonel Pickering.

Colonel Pickering is uncomfortable and is made even more so when Eliza asks if he will wish to continue their friendship now that the experiment is over. She thanks Colonel Pickering for teaching her good manners. She says that this was quite difficult for her when Higgins set such a bad example with his temper and his swearing. Colonel Pickering taught her what it meant to be a lady by calling her Miss Doolittle from the first day at Wimpole Street and by his general behaviour and good manners towards her. Pickering is touched while Higgins sits grinding his teeth in anger. She makes her point by saying she would like Pickering to call her Eliza, and Higgins to call her Miss Doolittle.

Higgins's predictions stem from his conceit.

Higgins says he will see her damned first. Eliza refuses to be drawn into a row with him and says that leaving Wimpole Street is the final stage in her break with her former life. Pickering is upset that she is not going back. Higgins predicts that without him she will be in the gutter again in three weeks. She reassures Pickering that she could not go back to her old ways but Higgins is delighted when Eliza lets out one of her old yells at the sight of her father as he enters from the balcony.

This shows that Mrs Higgins has accepted Eliza into her class.

Doolittle announces that he is on his way to church to be married to Eliza's stepmother, another result of joining the middle class. He asks Eliza to attend the wedding. She reluctantly agrees and goes off to get ready. Doolittle asks Pickering to go to the church with him to give him support. Mrs Higgins asks if she may go too and Doolittle says he would be honoured and she goes of to get ready, meeting Eliza on the way out and suggesting they travel together. Before he leaves with Doolittle, Colonel Pickering makes one more attempt to persuade Eliza to return to live at Wimpole Street.

COMMENT   Henry is very self-centred. He finds Eliza's leaving is causing him inconvenience.

Eliza is praising Pickering's gentlemanly behaviour and obviously making the point that Higgins's manners are appalling.

Eliza makes it clear that she considers Pickering to be

her friend when she asks him to call her Eliza and shows she requires some respect from Higgins when she says she wants him to call her Miss Doolittle.

There is humour in the irony (see Literary Terms) that Doolittle should find his good fortune such a burden. It is another example of Higgins's actions having unforeseen effects.

GLOSSARY
genteel respectable, well-mannered
worrited worried
acause because
Skilly a thin porridge or gruel
Char Bydis Charybdis, a dangerous monster in Greek legend who sat on a rock opposite another monster called Scylla. They represented alternate dangers and here Doolittle is making an amusing mistake
fire irons tools kept by the grate for tending a coal fire, a poker and tongs
tremenjous tremendous
brougham a one-horse carriage

[ELIZA AND HIGGINS]

(pp. 97–105)

When Eliza is left alone with Higgins she tries to avoid him but he confronts her and asks her if she is going to be reasonable now that she has had a bit of her own back. She says he only wants her to fetch and carry. Higgins says he does not intend to change and that he treats everyone exactly the same. Eliza tells him that she can bear to be treated badly but she cannot bear to be ignored or taken for granted. She says that he has no consideration for anyone.

Higgins admits he will miss Eliza.

Higgins finally admits that he will miss her, that she has become an important part of his life. Eliza accuses him of trying to manipulate her and says she will not care for anyone who does not care for her. Higgins says this is like trading in affection and he rejects it. He admires her spirit and independence and tells her he does not want anyone slaving after him. He does not regret causing her problems as he believes that nothing would get done if we worried too much about making trouble. Eliza feels she has somehow lost her independence, her ability to earn her own living, by becoming a lady. Higgins suggests that he could adopt her or she could marry Pickering. She rejects both of these ideas and mentions that she could have Freddy for a husband and he at least loves her. Higgins tells her that she has a sentimental attitude and that she may as well go and marry a common man who will be sentimental with her and beat her when he is drunk.

Eliza is determined not to go back to Wimpole Street. She says she will get a job teaching phonetics and will marry Freddy as soon as she is able to support him. At first Higgins scoffs at both of these ideas. He thinks Freddy is foolish and useless. However Eliza makes him really angry when she says she might join with his Hungarian ex-pupil. He almost strikes her and she realises she has hit him on a sensitive spot, his *Eliza finds* professional reputation. Eventually he says he is proud *Higgins's weak* of spirit and that now the three of them can live at *spot.* Wimpole Street on equal terms. When Mrs Higgins arrives, Eliza tells Henry she will not be seeing him again. He tries to ignore this and to involve her in some details about shopping but she replies quite firmly and leaves with Mrs Higgins, as Henry tells his mother that she is going to marry Freddy and roars with laughter.

COMMENT   Although Higgins admits he misses Eliza, he will not have anything to do with sentimentality. He wants a friendship of equals.

Eliza intends to support Freddy as she realises his upbringing has not prepared him for earning a living. This is a reversal of the expected roles of men and women.

TEST YOURSELF (Act V)

A Identify the speaker.

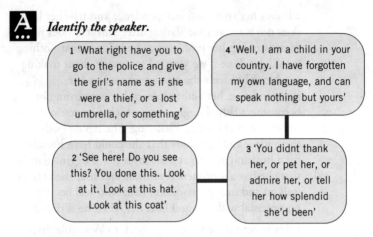

1 'What right have you to go to the police and give the girl's name as if she were a thief, or a lost umbrella, or something'

4 'Well, I am a child in your country. I have forgotten my own language, and can speak nothing but yours'

2 'See here! Do you see this? You done this. Look at it. Look at this hat. Look at this coat'

3 'You didnt thank her, or pet her, or admire her, or tell her how splendid she'd been'

Identify the person 'to whom' this comment refers.

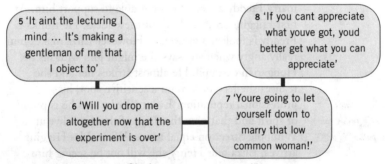

5 'It aint the lecturing I mind ... It's making a gentleman of me that I object to'

8 'If you cant appreciate what youve got, youd better get what you can appreciate'

6 'Will you drop me altogether now that the experiment is over'

7 'Youre going to let yourself down to marry that low common woman!'

Check your answers on page 64.

B Consider these issues.

a How Mrs Higgins reacts to Henry's treatment of Eliza.

b The way Alfred's confused sense of morality is used to create humour.

c Eliza seems to understand her situation far better than any of the 'educated' people around her.

d Whether Higgins really has been mean to Eliza, or whether this is simply his way of behaving to everyone.

e Eliza's reaction to her father's marriage announcement makes her sound like Higgins.

AFTERWORD

Shaw wrote the afterword to dispel any ideas that Eliza and Higgins would eventually marry. He presents a series of events which includes Colonel Pickering helping Eliza and Freddy to open a flower shop. He had called the play a romance (see Literary Terms) in the sense that it presented a series of unlikely events, not that it was a love story.

COMMENT It would be sheer sentimentality to suggest that Eliza would share her future with Higgins. Shaw's final comment is that 'Galatea never did quite like Pygmalion'; similarly Eliza does not really like Higgins. Freddy and Pickering deserve Eliza's affection whereas Higgins does not.

Shaw takes the opportunity to comment further upon the inadequacies and pretensions of the middle classes, as represented by the Eynsford-Hills. Freddy, though inept, survives through Eliza's success but this would seem a disgrace to his mother.

PART THREE

COMMENTARY

THEMES

MOVING UP THE SOCIAL LADDER

The title *Pygmalion* is taken from a Greek legend, in
which Pygmalion was the King of Cyprus. He fell in
love with a statue that he had made and prayed to the
goddess Aphrodite to give him a wife as beautiful as the
statue. She did more than this, as she gave life to the
statue. Pygmalion married the woman who was created;
her name was Galatea. This Greek myth serves as a
metaphor (see Literary Terms) for the action in the
play.

The 'Nature versus nurture' debate

The play reflects a debate that was taking place in
society at the time. Famous writers such as George
Bernard Shaw and H.G. Wells were part of a
movement which felt that people could rise above the
position into which they were born. Shaw explores this
idea in *Pygmalion*. The debate is often referred to as
Nature versus nurture. This marked a major change in
thinking from that of Victorian England. A basic belief
of the Victorians was:

* A person is born into a class and so belongs
  there. No one can move from one class to
  another

The new thinkers believed that
* A person is not defined by the position into which he
  is born
* Through education, social change can be achieved

Since 1870 basic education had been available for
all, for the first time. This led to people being
less likely to 'know their place' and to old ideas
being challenged. *Pygmalion* is part of that
challenge.

THE SCIENCE OF LANGUAGE

Shaw's play reflects the great interest in phonetics at this time.

There was great interest at the turn of the century in the idea of creating an alphabet which would allow English to be written down clearly, wherever in the country it was spoken. At the turn of the century there was neither television nor radio and so accents in different parts of the country were very strong. Shaw wanted an alphabet which could be universal and so make communication easier. At this time there was much interest among academics in the idea of making everything fit a pattern. This follows the thinking of the great Victorian scientist, Charles Darwin, whose *Theory of Evolution* allowed all living things on Earth to be classified. As part of this thinking, Shaw tried very hard to change the spelling system of the English language. He felt that a more scientific approach was needed and that the spelling system used (the one we still use today) was hopelessly confusing. He gave a famous demonstration of this by showing how the word *fish* could be spelt *ghoti* as follows:

> *gh* in laugh gives the sound F
> *o* in women gives the sound I
> *ti* in nation gives the sound SH

Shaw makes the invention of a phonetic system of writing one of the central ideas in *Pygmalion*. Henry Higgins is very successful because of his ability to reproduce any sound that is made in any accent. He does this through the use of an alphabet which has a symbol for every different sound that the human voice can make.

WOMEN'S SUFFRAGE

Shaw was a member of the Fabian Society and was involved in the Suffragette movement. This sought the vote for women and more acceptance of the equality of the sexes. He wrote many strongly worded letters on the subject and helped to raise public awareness of the Suffragette cause. When women protested about not having the right to vote they were arrested. They often went on hunger strike in prison and the authorities insisted that the women should be force-fed. A tube was pushed against her will into a woman's mouth or up her nose and liquid food poured down it. This killed many women and was denounced by Shaw as being totally inhumane. In a letter to *The Times* in 1913 Shaw wrote:

Shaw denounced the brutal treatment of Suffragettes.

> I contend that this forcible feeding is illegal ... if the Government wants to break people's teeth with chisels, and force food into the lungs and run the risk of killing them, to inflict what is unquestionably torture on them, their business is to bring in a bill legalising these operations. They have no shame in doing it without the law. Why should they be ashamed of doing it with the law?

Shaw's attitude to the equality of men and women is revealed through the way he has created the part of Eliza. Female characters in plays of the period were either old women or helpless girls who needed a man to rescue them. In *Pygmalion*, Shaw moves well away from this typical Victorian melodrama and makes Eliza a free-thinking character. Even though her speech changes, she does not become a mere reflection of Higgins but stands up for herself and wins her independence.

THE IDLE CLASS

When the play was first performed on the London stage in 1914, England was a very different country from the one it is today. Over three-quarters of the nation's wealth was owned by only 1 per cent of the population. There was a huge gulf between the rich and

the poor and this gap was very difficult to bridge. The
extremely wealthy upper classes owned most of the land
in the country and made such a good living from their
inherited money that they did not have to work. These
people are satirised (see Literary Terms) in the embassy
scene in *Pygmalion*, Act III, where they are shown to be
stupid and easily fooled.

The less prosperous middle classes looked up to their
wealthier superiors and often attempted to copy their
behaviour. The absurd speech of Freddy and Clara's
readiness to adopt any new way of speaking that might
be fashionable are examples of this.

EDUCATION FOR ALL

George Bernard Shaw believed strongly that everyone
should have the right to an education. He felt that
educating the population would bring about a better
and fairer society. In *Pygmalion*, a simple flower girl is
able to pass herself off as a duchess. Shaw felt that
people should not be limited by birth, but should be
given the opportunity to improve themselves. His aims
for the Fabian Society were: 'to establish equality as the
universal relation between citizens without distinction
of sex, colour, occupation, age, talent, character,
heredity or what not', and education was central to
these aims.

STRUCTURE

The play moves between four major locations as shown
in the table overleaf. The scenes are mostly domestic
and tension is developed through the interplay between
Eliza, Higgins and Pickering.

Dramatic tension is also introduced and sustained
through the experiment to pass Eliza off as a duchess.
There is an anti-climax (see Literary Terms) once the

TABLE OF LOCATIONS

	Covent Garden	Wimpole Street	Mrs Higgins's flat	The Embassy	In the street	
ACT I	Higgins and Pickering meet	Eliza - a poor and dirty flower girl	Eynsford Hill Family			
ACT II	Higgins and Pickering make a bet	Eliza bathed and changed - lessons begin	Mrs Pearce not in favour of the plan	Alfred Doolittle tries his luck		
ACT III	Higgins shows off Eliza	Eliza not quite ready	Ladies impressed by Eliza - Freddy in love	Mrs Higgins worried about Eliza		SIX MONTHS
	Higgins wins his bet	Eliza a success				
ACT IV	Higgins surprised by Eliza's anger	Eliza angry - feels useless and discarded				
	Eliza runs off with Freddy	Freddy waiting in the street to see Eliza				
ACT V	Higgins fails to persuade Eliza to return	Eliza to set up on her own and marry Freddy	Doolittle now rich - his wedding day	Mrs Higgins has taken Eliza in		

The play moves between four major locations as shown in the table. The scenes are mostly domestic and tension is developed through the interplay between Eliza, Higgins and Pickering. Dramatic tension is also introduced and sustained through the experiment to pass Eliza off as a duchess. There is an anti-climax once the bet has been won, and this leads to the drama of the emotional issues between Higgins and Eliza.

bet has been won, and this leads to the drama of the emotional issues between Higgins and Eliza.

The two characters of Eliza and Higgins are used by Shaw to put forward his views on his favourite subjects:
- The emancipation of women
- The breaking down of class barriers through education
- The development of a universal alphabet

CHARACTERS

HENRY HIGGINS

Talented
Confident
Attention-seeking
Single-minded
Tactless

He treats people as things upon which to experiment.

Henry Higgins is an intelligent, single-minded man. He is an expert in the field of phonetics, but he has allowed his work to become an obsession. Higgins is an example of a middle-class eccentric. He shows little sensitivity towards the feelings of others and many people, including his own mother, find him rude. Higgins likes to be the centre of attention and is a show-off. His desire to impress an audience sometimes leads him to behave quite tactlessly and his determination to succeed makes him seem ill-mannered.

Though Higgins does treat people badly, he does not intend to cause offence. He tries to explain this to Eliza in Act V, but his notion of treating everyone the same on all occasions does not excuse his bad behaviour. He is simply not very good at relating to people on a personal level and appears truly confident only when talking about his pet subject.

He is proud of his reputation and jealous of anyone who might prove better than him. This partly explains how annoyed he is when he hears that Eliza is to set herself up as a teacher of phonetics. He threatens to wring her neck when she says that she will teach his methods to the Hungarian. He is proud of having created the new Eliza and states that his work is more important than any one person.

Higgins does not feel that he has to behave according to anyone else's rules and his own views on life seem quite cold and impersonal. He bullies those who do not see things so clearly as he does and is actually quite proud of his lack of sentimentality.

Higgins is said to have been based on a real-life phonetics scholar, Henry Sweet.

ELIZA DOOLITTLE

Quick-witted
Ignorant
Moral
Elegant

At the start of the play Eliza is naïve, simple and ignorant. She has grown up in poverty and has had to fend for herself. This has made her independent and able to look after herself. Despite her rough upbringing she has a strong sense of morality. She values her good name and is appalled at being thought of as a 'bad girl'. Unlike many girls in her situation, she has avoided the traps of crime and prostitution.

Eliza is ambitious to improve herself and is willing to grasp the first decent opportunity that arises. She is sensitive, as she shows in Act I (the Covent Garden scene) where she takes offence at the suggestion that she is behaving improperly.

As soon as she is presented with an opportunity, Eliza proves that she is quick to learn. She rapidly becomes a proficient student and the speed with which she learns astonishes even the cynical Higgins. Although she shows great strength of character and initiative, she remains vulnerable. We see this in her reactions to the insensitivity of Higgins's treatment.

Her need for affection leads her to respond to Freddy. He is an unlikely match for her and in fact she is going to have to look after him. In the final scene her grace and dignity show themselves clearly.

ALFRED DOOLITTLE

Doolittle is seen a lovable rogue. His upside-down morality is a source of amusement to the gentlemen, especially Higgins. He is amoral and quite shameless in his attempt at blackmail. He is happy in his station in life, even though he has to 'touch' others for money. He does not want responsibility and is proud of being one of the undeserving poor. He insists on taking £5 rather than £10 as he feels that £10 is so much money that it could not be squandered.

Lovable rogue
Amoral,
Shameless

It is ironic (see Literary Terms) that his skill in begging for money and his eloquence when putting forward his odd views should be the cause of him coming into wealth. Once he is wealthy, he complains bitterly of his new responsibilities. He gains a host of new relatives, all of whom expect his financial support. He feels that he will have to learn to speak in middle-class English.

COLONEL PICKERING

Pickering is an old-fashioned gentleman and scholar who has a military background. He has spent many years in India and is an expert in languages. He behaves like a kind uncle towards Eliza and she appreciates that he always treats her like a lady. However, he is drawn in by Higgins's enthusiasm and cannot resist the excitement of the bet.

Sensitive
Gentlemanly
Schoolboyish

He acts as a foil to Higgins's insensitive behaviour of others and often attempts to restrain the professor. There is something of the schoolboy in him and he is not always aware of the effects of the experiment upon Eliza. On occasion he talks to Higgins about Eliza as though she were not there when she is actually in the room.

MRS HIGGINS

Mrs Higgins is the mother of Henry. She is a cultured lady who has surrounded herself with fine things. An intelligent woman, she is well aware of her son's bad behaviour and shortcomings, and treats him quite firmly. As his mother, she understands his habits and rash ways.

Mrs Higgins is concerned about what will happen to Eliza when the experiment is over. She gives Eliza shelter when the girl runs away from Higgins. She shows her generous and open-minded nature when she

- Entertains the Eynsford Hills, even though they are not fashionable
- Is prepared to attend Alfred's wedding

Cultured
Intelligent
Generous
Conscientious

Although she is wealthy she does not behave snobbishly.

MINOR CHARACTERS

MRS EYNSFORD HILL

A middle-class lady who has fallen on hard times. She does not have the money to keep up with polite society. She still behaves as though she is a member of Society and tries to develop friendships that may do her and her children some good.

CLARA

Clara Eynsford Hill is a snobbish, gullible girl. She is preoccupied with the latest fashions but shows that she has no judgement at all when it comes to deciding what is actually in fashion. She is easily fooled into thinking that Eliza's strange vocabulary is 'the new small talk'.

FREDDY

Weak and ineffectual

Freddy Eynsford Hill is a weak and ineffectual young man. He proves early on in Act I that he is not much use for anything when he is unable even to order a taxi. When one does arrive, he lets Eliza take it from him.

Higgins says that Freddy could not even get a job as an errand boy, even if he had the guts to try for it.

He falls in love with Eliza and provides much needed affection for her. Eliza realises that she will have to support him as he was not brought up to work.

As Shaw comments in the Afterword: 'A clerkship at thirty shillings a week was beneath Freddy's dignity, and extremely distasteful to him besides.' What Freddy really wanted was a job with a nice title and income, but entailing no work or effort. In Freddy, Shaw makes fun of upper middle-class affectations, with his 'righto' and 'ripping' slang.

MRS PEARCE Like Mrs Higgins, she is a sensible woman who treats people decently. She tries hard to cope with Higgins's behaviour, commenting tactfully on his bad language and poor table manners. She sees problems ahead for Eliza because of the experiment and is genuinely concerned for the girl.

LANGUAGE & STYLE

George Bernard Shaw was very interested in the introduction of a phonetic alphabet which would have allowed all the sounds in spoken English to be written down without confusion. To illustrate this, Shaw set the play in London and chose to use the heavy accent of a cockney flower girl.

Though the play was intended for performance, Shaw always has an eye on the fact that it would also be read. The attempt in Act I to represent Eliza's accent in

*Shaw attempted
to simplify
spelling, refusing
to use any
apostrophes, e.g.
'dont', 'wont',
'youre'.*

written form shows this. Shaw uses the idea that Eliza's speech cannot be written clearly whilst still retaining all its sounds, as an example of the inadequacy of our twenty-six-letter alphabet.

The play features several accents
- Eliza and Doolittle: broad London accent, using some words of dialect
- Higgins, Pickering and Mrs Higgins: formal, standard English, with emphasis on 'correct' pronunciation
- Freddy Eynsford Hill: silly, pretentious, would-be upper-class, using phrases such as 'Ahdedo'
- Mrs Eynsford Hill and Clara: ready to use whatever new words or pronunciation may be thought to be fashionable

Shaw also looks at the reaction to bad language. Higgins is supposedly a gentleman, yet he swears in front of Eliza, his mother and Mrs Eynsford Hill. Even the common Eliza does not do this, perhaps hinting that Shaw felt the middle classes to be hypocritical in the standards they applied to others.

Above all, the play uses language to show that the way a person speaks cannot define the sort of person he/she is. The polite society of the time judged people by the way they spoke and Shaw shows this to be foolish. The character who speaks with the most upper-class accent is the foolish Freddy; the two commonest speakers, Doolittle and Eliza, prove to be much more interesting characters altogether.

Shaw's humour lies in the fact that though Eliza has learned to pronounce words correctly, her *choice* of words is often totally inappropriate.

PART FOUR

Study Skills

How to use quotations

One of the secrets of success in writing essays is the
way you use quotations. There are five basic principles:
- Put inverted commas at the beginning and end of the
  quotation
- Write the quotation exactly as it appears in the
  original
- Do not use a quotation that repeats what you have
  just written
- Use the quotation so that it fits into your sentence
- Keep the quotation as short as possible

Quotations should be used to develop the line of
thought in your essays.

Your comment should not duplicate what is in the
quotation. For example:

**Eliza asks whether her clothes belong to her or to Colonel
Pickering, 'Do my clothes belong to me or to Colonel Pickering?'**

Far more effective is to write:

**Eliza is confused and asks, 'Do my clothes belong to me or to
Colonel Pickering?'**

The most sophisticated way of using the writer's words
is to embed them into your sentence:

**The fact that Higgins says, 'shall we throw her out of the
window?' in front of Eliza, indicates that he has a cruel sense of
humour.**

When you use quotations in this way, you are
demonstrating the ability to use text as evidence to
support your ideas - not simply including words from
the original to prove you have read it.

Everyone writes differently. Work through the suggestions given here and adapt the advice to suit your own style and interests. This will improve your essay-writing skills and allow your personal voice to emerge.

The following points indicate in ascending order the skills of essay writing:

- Picking out one or two facts about the story and adding the odd detail
- Writing about the text by retelling the story
- Retelling the story and adding a quotation here and there
- Organising an answer which explains what is happening in the text and giving quotations to support what you write
....
- Writing in such a way as to show that you have thought about the intentions of the writer of the text and that you understand the techniques used
- Writing at some length, giving your viewpoint on the text and commenting by picking out details to support your views
- Looking at the text as a work of art, demonstrating clear critical judgement and explaining to the reader of your essay how the enjoyment of the text is assisted by literary devices, linguistic effects and psychological insights; showing how the text relates to the time when it was written

The dotted line above represents the division between lower- and higher-level grades. Higher-level performance begins when you start to consider your response as a reader of the text. The highest level is reached when you offer an enthusiastic personal response and show how this piece of literature is a product of its time.

Coursework | Set aside an hour or so at the start of your work to plan
essay | what you have to do.

- List all the points you feel are needed to cover the task. Collect page references of information and quotations that will support what you have to say. A helpful tool is the highlighter pen: this saves painstaking copying and enables you to target precisely what you want to use.
- Focus on what you consider to be the main points of the essay. Try to sum up your argument in a single sentence, which could be the closing sentence of your essay. Depending on the essay title, it could be a statement about a character: Although Eliza has lived in poverty all her life, she has a clearly developed sense of right and wrong; an opinion about a setting: The use of Covent Garden Market allows all the characters to meet up, as it is one of the few places in which the different levels of society might have come across one another; or a judgement on a theme: I think that the main theme of *Pygmalion* is that no one is born to be anything. People are what their environment makes them: a duchess born into poverty would not behave like a duchess and a flower girl born into a wealthy family would not behave like a common street urchin.
- Make a short essay plan. Use the first paragraph to introduce the argument you wish to make. In the following paragraphs develop this argument with details, examples and other possible points of view. Sum up your argument in the last paragraph. Check you have answered the question.
- Write the essay, remembering all the time the central point you are making.
- On completion, go back over what you have written to eliminate careless errors and improve expression. Read it aloud to yourself, or, if you are feeling more confident, to a relative or friend.

If you can, try to type your essay using a word processor. This will allow you to correct and improve your writing without spoiling its appearance.

Examination essay

The essay written in an examination often carries more marks than the coursework essay even though it is written under considerable time pressure.

In the revision period, build up notes on various aspects of the text you are using. Fortunately, in acquiring this set of York Notes on *Pygmalion,* you have made a prudent beginning! York Notes are set out to give you vital information and help you to construct your personal overview of the text.

Make notes with appropriate quotations about the key issues of the set text. Go into the examination knowing your text and having a clear set of opinions about it.

In most English Literature examinations you can take in copies of your set books. This in an enormous advantage although it may lull you into a false sense of security. Beware! There is simply not enough time in an examination to read the book from scratch.

In the examination

- Read the question paper carefully and remind yourself what you have to do.
- Look at the questions on your set texts to select the one that most interests you and mentally work out the points you wish to stress.
- Remind yourself of the time available and how you are going to use it.
- Briefly map out a short plan in note form that will keep your writing on track and illustrate the key argument you want to make.
- Then set about writing it.
- When you have finished, check through to eliminate errors.

To summarise, these are the keys to success

- **Know the play**
- **Have a clear understanding of and opinions on the storyline, characters, setting, themes and writer's concerns**
- **Select the right material**
- **Plan and write a clear response, continually bearing the question in mind**

SAMPLE ESSAY PLAN

A typical essay question on *Pygmalion* is followed by a sample essay plan in note form. This does not present the only answer to the question, merely one answer. Do not be afraid to include your own ideas, and leave out some of those in the sample! Remember that quotations are essential to prove and illustrate the points you make.

What changes do we see in Eliza during the course of the play?

Look through the play for changes in her outward appearance (shown in stage directions), her manners and her language, and in others' reaction to her. You can either treat this, theme by theme, or chronologically as shown here.

Part 1   Refer to details from stage directions for Act I about her dirty, scruffy appearance, as a flower girl.

She is loud with a very strong cockney dialect. Give example of her dialect e.g. 'Will ye-oo py me f'them?' She is almost begging in her manner as she presses the public to buy flowers, but she is confident and good at her job. Eliza defends her reputation and shows pride. She knows her rights and does not back down easily. She shows her ignorance when she thinks the man taking down notes is a policeman. Taking the cab home shows she would like a better life.

Part 2   At Higgins's laboratory in Act II, she shows ambition, wants to better herself through speech lessons. Not stupid, she questions the intentions of the men. Quite aware that men might want to trick her; suspicious of the offer of a chocolate. Ignorance shown when she sees the bathroom and thinks the bath is for boiling clothes. Appearance changes dramatically once she is clean and wearing new clothes. Father doesn't recognise her. Works hard and shows aptitude in the first lessons.

Part 3   At Mrs Higgins's flat, she has learned to pronounce and present herself well, but the content of her conversation is still lower class, e.g. discussion of her aunt's death.

Part 4   Her appearance at the embassy is a great success, she has learned her lessons well. Is mistaken for a princess.

Part 5   Back at Wimpole Street wants to be valued as a person and not just part of a bet; still strong-willed, prepared to defend herself; shows pride. Still vulnerable and concerned about her future. Realises that being educated to be a lady does not fit her to earn a living. Shows need for affection – Freddy. Asserts her independence by leaving Wimpole Street.

Part 6   At Mrs Higgins's flat, shows dignity and restraint. Does not rise to Higgins's provocation. Neatly plays off Pickering against Higgins – shows sophistication. Realises how much she has changed but that she is still not accepted as a lady. Stands up to the bullying of Higgins and so impresses him. Decides to marry Freddy and look after him – a reversal of the male/female roles.

Conclusion   Changes in manners, language, appearance. But, unlike middle-class women, will still have to make her own way in life. Her original ambition, self-reliance and energy will enable her to do this. She has come a long way from the common flower girl but still retains the honesty and sensitivity which made her appealing in the first place.

FURTHER QUESTIONS

1 How does Shaw present class differences in the play?
   You should refer to three of the characters.
2 The women in *Pygmalion* seem more sensible than
   the men. Discuss this, bearing in mind that Shaw
   was a strong supporter of the Suffragette Movement.
3 Compare the attitudes of
   • Higgins
   • Colonel Pickering
   • Alfred Doolittle
     towards Eliza.
4 Discuss the nature of the relationship between
   Higgins and Eliza.

PART FIVE

CULTURAL CONNECTIONS

BROADER PERSPECTIVES

The play has four main themes which make it still relevant today:
- The role of women in society
- The importance of class background
- Education as a key to progress
- Different kinds of language

Some other sources which deal with the same issues are books: you will probably enjoy reading *Decline and Fall* (1928) by Evelyn Waugh – a satirical attack upon the class system in England; and John Braine's *Room at the Top* (1957) – about the rise of an ambitious young man with working-class origins.

There are a number of plays and films which depict similar themes. First of all there is *My Fair Lady* – the musical version of *Pygmalion*. *Shirley Valentine* by Willy Russell is a film – and play – in which an ordinary housewife escapes from the drudgery of her existence. *Educating Rita*, also by Willy Russell, is a film and play dealing with the education of a working-class woman and the changes that this brings about. And predating Shaw's *Pygmalion* by a dozen years is *The Admirable Crichton*, a play written by J.M. Barrie, and first performed in 1902, in which an upper-class household is shipwrecked. The butler, Crichton, takes charge as he turns out to be the most capable person. This was later made into a very successful film.

alliteration a series of similar consonant sounds, usually at the beginning of words. Alliteration is a *figure of speech* used to enrich the sound of a piece of writing or to give stress to a particular point

anti-climax a point where the plot does not achieve the expected climax, but becomes dull and digressive

irony saying one thing whilst you mean another. Ironic statements are often made by characters who do not realise the full impact of what has been said. It can be used to achieve humour or pathos

melodrama a piece of work, often a play, which relies upon sensational happenings and simple good/evil characters. Melodrama became very popular in Victorian England and such melodramas featured wicked villains plotting to trap virtuous maidens. A

hero usually came to her rescue at the end of the piece

metaphor a parallel image giving deeper meaning to the original subject-matter

pathos a quality which invokes pity and sadness in the reader or listener. It was used a great deal in Victorian literature and writers such as Charles Dickens were very skilful in using it to control the emotions of the reader

pun a play on words in which a word with more than one meaning is deliberately used, usually to create humour

romance a work featuring unrealistic characters and storylines. Romances often deal with deeds of bravery in the pursuit of love and feature knights, dragons etc. Shaw calls *Pygmalion* a romance, but only in the sense that it is far-fetched and unlikely to happen

satire the intentional use of humour to make a vice or folly appear ridiculous

TEST ANSWERS

TEST YOURSELF (Act I)

A 1 Mrs Eynsford Hill (The Mother)
... 2 Higgins
3 Eliza
4 Pickering
5 The Taximan
6 Higgins
7 Clara
8 Pickering (The Gentleman)

TEST YOURSELF (Act II)

A 1 Higgins
... 2 Higgins
3 Mrs Pearce
4 Alfred Doolittle
5 Pickering
6 Alfred Doolittle
7 Pickering
8 Higgins

TEST YOURSELF (Act III)

A 1 Mrs Higgins
... 2 Higgins
3 Eliza

4 Higgins
5 Mrs Eynsford Hill
6 Mrs Higgins

TEST YOURSELF (Act IV)

A 1 Higgins
... 2 Pickering
3 Eliza
4 Eliza
5 Freddy
6 Higgins
7 Eliza
8 Freddy

TEST YOURSELF (Act V)

A 1 Mrs Higins
... 2 Alfred Doolittle
3 Mrs Higgins
4 Eliza
5 Higgins
6 Pickering
7 Alfred Doolittle
8 Eliza